DATE DUE

The Best Book of
Mummies

Philip Steele

KINGFISHER
BOSTON

Author: Philip Steele
Consultant: Dr Anne Millard
Editor: Vicky Weber
Illustrators: Vanessa Card, Angus
 McBride, Nicki Palin, Mark Peppe
Art Editor: Christina Fraser
Cover Designer: Mike Buckley
Production Controller: Eliot Sedman

Contents

KINGFISHER
a Houghton Mifflin Company imprint
222 Berkeley Street
Boston, Massachusetts 02116
www.houghtonmifflinbooks.com

First published in 1998
10 9 8 7 6 5 4 3 2 1

2TR/0705/SHEN/PICA(PICA)/126.6MA

LIBRARY OF CONGRESS CATALOGING-IN-PUBLICATION DATA
Steele, Philip.
    The best book of mummies / Philip Steele.—1st ed.
        p.   cm.
    Includes index.
    1. Mummies—Egypt—Juvenile literature. I. Title.
DT62.M7S8   1998
932—dc21   97-42593   CIP AC

ISBN 0-7534-5873-X
ISBN 978-07534-5873-0

Printed in Taiwan

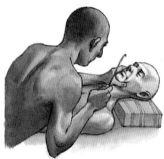

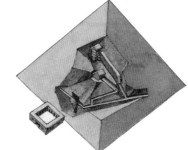

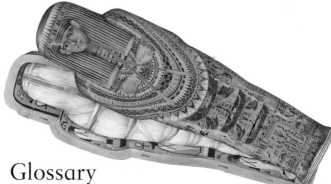

A secret tomb

Imagine opening up the secret tomb of someone who has been dead for thousands of years. You peer into the darkness. Is that a glint of gold? You hold up a candle. The chamber is filled with treasures. Beyond, there are other chambers, too. In one of them you hope to discover the coffin of a dead pharaoh, a king of ancient Egypt. What will be inside the coffin? A crumbling skeleton? Probably not. The bodies of the pharaohs were specially preserved, so that they would last forever.

Face of a mummy

Meet Seti I, an Egyptian king. Seti died around 3,300 years ago! When he died, his body was made into a mummy, to preserve it and keep it whole. Sometimes dead bodies become mummies naturally, dried out in sand or frozen in ice. But the ancient Egyptians made mummies on purpose.

The pharaohs

Why did the ancient Egyptians turn bodies into mummies? They believed a dead person needed his or her body to enjoy life in the Next World. It was especially important for the pharaohs to be made into mummies. The pharaohs were powerful kings who ruled Egypt for thousands of years. The ancient Egyptians believed that the pharaohs were living gods. If the magical link between the pharaohs and the Next World were broken, then the whole Earth would vanish into darkness and chaos.

Gifts for a living god

The pharaoh and his queen received all types of gifts from people of other lands—ivory elephant tusks, animal skins, spices, gold, and jewels. Riches like these were placed in the pharaoh's tomb so that he could use them when he reached the Next World.

Crook

Flail

Scepters carried by the pharaoh

The land of Egypt

The pharaohs ruled over the green lands around the Nile river and the dusty deserts beyond. They built great cities, tombs, and temples.

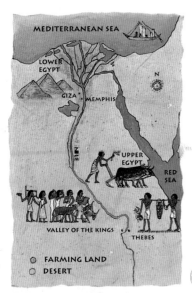

MEDITERRANEAN SEA

LOWER EGYPT

GIZA · MEMPHIS

N

NILE

UPPER EGYPT

RED SEA

VALLEY OF THE KINGS

THEBES

○ FARMING LAND
○ DESERT

The Egyptian people

People believed that the pharaoh protected Egypt from disaster, but really it was the hard work of thousands of ordinary people that kept the kingdom going.

The pharaoh was at the head of Egyptian society. Beneath him were other members of the royal family. Below them were the nobles, followed by the wealthy middle classes. At the bottom were the peasants who farmed the land. Normally, only rich people could afford to have their bodies turned into mummies.

Top people

The royal family lived in palaces, ate fine food, and enjoyed hunting and music. Some nobles became royal officials, such as governors. Others were generals or priests.

Hard workers

Most Egyptians had to work hard. Farmers planted crops and looked after cattle. They also had to help build huge temples or tombs.

Slaves were usually foreign prisoners of war. They were often used to do dangerous jobs, such as mining.

Peasants, unskilled workers, slaves

Pharaoh,
queen,
the royal
family

In the middle

Engineers, architects, doctors,
and skilled craftworkers were well
respected and often rich. So were
the government officials, clerks,
and writers, known as scribes.

Nobles,
governors,
generals,
chief priests

Scribes,
doctors,
engineers,
merchants,
top craft-
workers

Professional
mourners,
minor priests
and priestesses,
craftworkers

Soldiers,
sailors,
household
servants,
performers,
dancers

9

Gods and goddesses

The ancient Egyptians worshiped hundreds of gods and goddesses.

Nut and **Geb**
Sky goddess (covered in stars) and god of the Earth

Ra (or **Re**)
God of the Sun

Osiris
God of death and rebirth

Isis
Mother goddess, wife of Osiris

Anubis
God of burial and embalmer

River

Atum

Hathor

Ferryman

The Next World

The ancient Egyptians believed that when they died they would travel to the Next World, the Kingdom of Osiris. They believed this kingdom was a wonderful place, and that whoever managed to reach it would live forever. However, the journey to the Next World was long and hard. On the journey, the dead needed food and drink. Their bodies had to be whole and strong. And the priests had to chant spells to protect them.

eth
od of chaos
nd confusion

Horus
Sky god, protector
of pharaohs

Amun
Creator god and
god of Thebes

Hathor
Goddess of
love and beauty

Thoth
God of writing
and knowledge

Judges   Weighing of the heart   Kingdom of Osiris

A difficult journey

he dead person asks a
rryman to help him cross
river into the Next World.
hen he must pass through
ven closely guarded gates.

He must fight snakes and
crocodiles, and evil gods try
to trap him in a net. But he
also gets help from the god
Atum, and food and water
from Hathor. He must then

face 42 judges before his
heart is weighed against the
feather of truth. If his heart
is heavy with sin, he will be
gobbled up by a monster.
If it is light, he will be saved.

Making a mummy

Welcome to the necropolis, the city of the dead! Here, the people who turned dead bodies into mummies worked. The skills of embalming, or mummy making, were passed on from father to son. Embalmers learned how to remove a body's insides, dry it with salty crystals, then bandage it from head to toe. As they worked, a priest chanted prayers, or spells, from the Book of the Dead, to protect the dead person on his or her journey to the Next World.

Book of the Dead
The Book of the Dead contained more than 200 spells in Egyptian picture writing, called hieroglyphs.

A grisly job

1▶ First, the embalmers washed the dead person's body with water or sweet-smelling palm oil.

2▶ The brain was pulled out through the nose, bit by bit, using a long bronze hook.

3▶ The heart was left in the body, but the intestines, liver, lungs, and stomach were cut out. They were dried in a kind of salt, called natron. Then, they were covered with gum taken from trees, bandaged, and placed in special jars.

Priest wearing mask of jackal-headed god Anubis

4◀ The body was put in a bath of natron to dry it. After 40 days, it was taken out. Its insides were stuffed with linen cloth, sand, or sawdust. Sometimes, the bandaged intestines, liver, stomach, and lungs were put back inside.

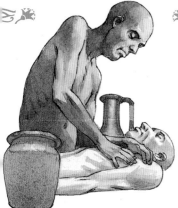

6 A charm was put over the hole where the body was cut open. The eye of the god Horus kept out evil spirits.

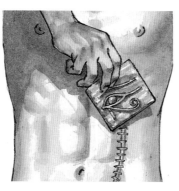

5 Gum and many different oils were rubbed into the body's dry skin. This softened it and made it smell better!

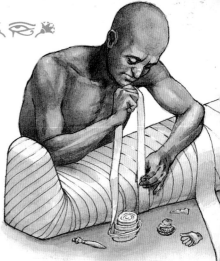

7 The body was wrapped in linen bandages, and lucky charms were placed between the layers.

8 A mask made of gold, or painted linen or plaster, was placed over the head and shoulders of the body.

9 The body was put in a human-shaped wooden coffin, covered with paintings and magic spells.

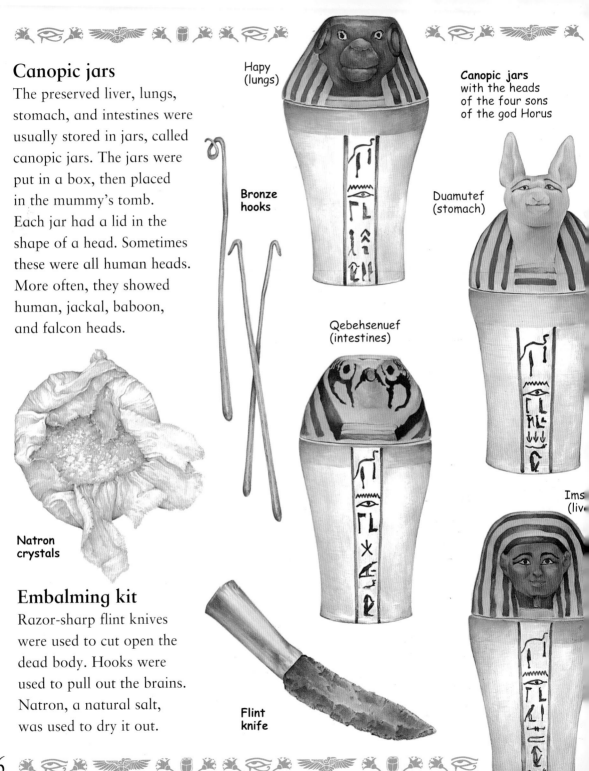

Canopic jars

The preserved liver, lungs, stomach, and intestines were usually stored in jars, called canopic jars. The jars were put in a box, then placed in the mummy's tomb. Each jar had a lid in the shape of a head. Sometimes these were all human heads. More often, they showed human, jackal, baboon, and falcon heads.

Natron crystals

Embalming kit

Razor-sharp flint knives were used to cut open the dead body. Hooks were used to pull out the brains. Natron, a natural salt, was used to dry it out.

Hapy (lungs)

Bronze hooks

Canopic jars with the heads of the four sons of the god Horus

Duamutef (stomach)

Qebehsenuef (intestines)

Ims (liv

Flint knife

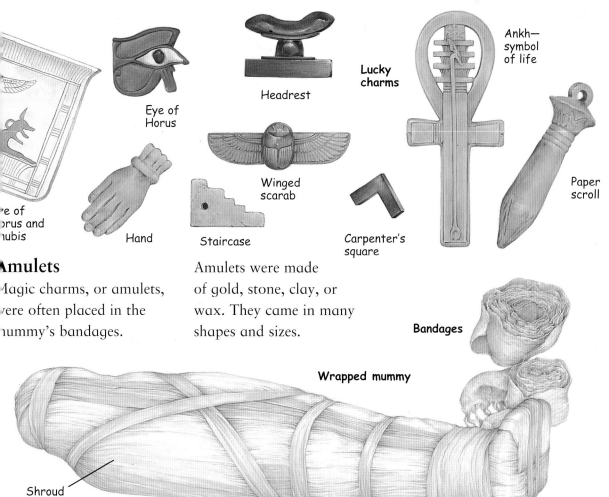

Eye of Horus

Headrest

Ankh— symbol of life

Winged scarab

Paper scroll

...e of ...rus and ...ubis

Hand

Staircase

Carpenter's square

Amulets

Magic charms, or amulets, were often placed in the mummy's bandages.

Amulets were made of gold, stone, clay, or wax. They came in many shapes and sizes.

Bandages

Wrapped mummy

Shroud

All wrapped up

A mummy's bandages were made of linen, never wool. The holiest bandages came from clothes that had been placed on the statues of gods in temples. The final layer was often a large sheet, or a shroud. Bandaging a mummy took 15 days.

Cat

Dog

Animal mummies

The Egyptians believed that many animals were holy or sacred. These animals were often made into mummies, just like humans. So were favorite family pets.

A funeral procession

A funeral procession is winding its way from the city of Thebes along the banks of the Nile river. Slowly, it climbs toward the edge of the desert, where a tomb has been carved in the rocky cliffs. Oxen haul the coffin over the stony ground on a boat-shaped sledge. Meanwhile, priests sprinkle milk and burn sweet-smelling incense. Women weep and wail as the procession passes by.

Opening of the mout

At a special ceremony, the priests "opened the mouth" of the mummy so the dead person could speak and move in the Next World.

Funeral boats

Sometimes, mummies were
carried on models of boats
or shown on a boat in a
painting in their tomb. This
was a symbol of the journey
by water to meet Osiris.

Coffins and cases

In the early days of ancient Egypt people were buried in pits in the desert. The hot sand soon dried out their bodies naturally. Later, the Egyptians buried bodies in simple reed and wooden coffins, but these bodies soon turned into skeletons. Around 4,600 years ago the Egyptians began to embalm bodies. Embalming continued for almost 3,000 years.

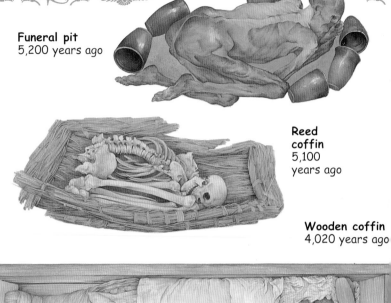

Funeral pit
5,200 years ago

Reed coffin
5,100 years ago

Wooden coffin
4,020 years ago

Mummy cases

Later, mummies were put into human-shaped coffins, or cases. The golden coffin below was made for a priestess from Thebes. Mummy cases were often covered in magic spells to keep the mummy safe.

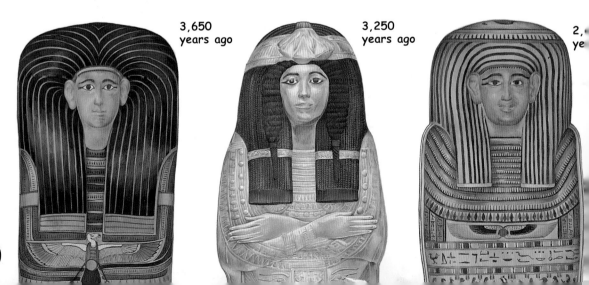

3,650 years ago

3,250 years ago

2,
ye

Nest of coffins

The body of the pharaoh Tutankhamen was protected by a nest of human-shaped mummy cases. The cases were put inside a big stone box called a sarcophagus. Each mummy case was decorated with gold and jewels. The mummy itself was wearing a beautiful mask made from solid gold. The coffins all provided a home for Tutankhamen's spirit, or ka.

When the Romans ruled Egypt, the paintings on coffins were more realistic.

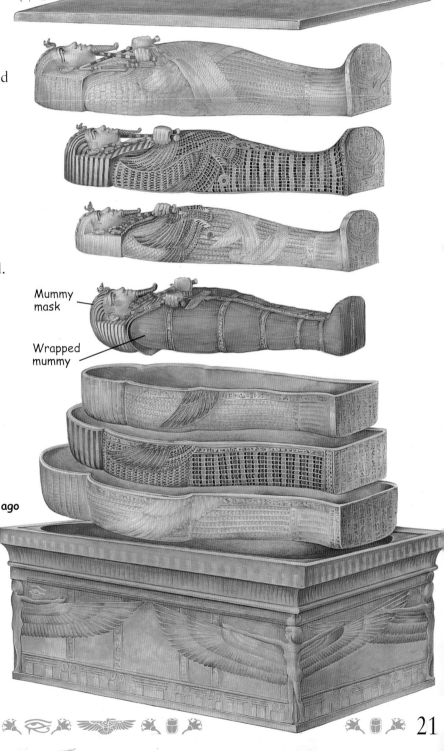

Mummy mask

Wrapped mummy

1,875 years ago

Food for the dead

Food and drink were left in tombs for the ka, or spirit, of the dead person. People believed that the ka needed these for nourishment. In the tomb of the young pharaoh Tutankhamen, archaeologists found 116 baskets of fruit and 40 jars of wine, as well as boxes of roasted meat and bread.

Duck

Goose

Wine

Rush container

Bread

Figs

Model servants

Little statues were often placed in tombs, too. A spell would make them come alive so they could work for the dead person in the Next World. Some figures looked lifelike. Others were shaped like tiny mummies and were called shabtis.

Sailing boat

Lady's maid

Threshing

Plowing

Mummy-shaped shabti figures

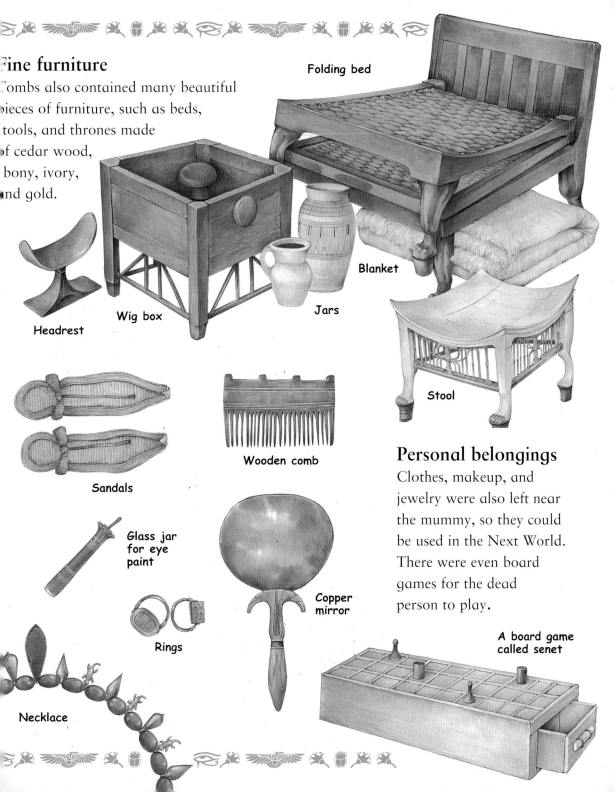

Fine furniture

Tombs also contained many beautiful pieces of furniture, such as beds, stools, and thrones made of cedar wood, ebony, ivory, and gold.

Folding bed

Blanket

Headrest

Wig box

Jars

Stool

Sandals

Wooden comb

Glass jar for eye paint

Rings

Copper mirror

Necklace

Personal belongings

Clothes, makeup, and jewelry were also left near the mummy, so they could be used in the Next World. There were even board games for the dead person to play.

A board game called senet

A mummy's tomb

Over thousands of years rich Egyptians built different types of tombs for their mummies. Most mummies were buried in underground chambers. Some of these were carved out of solid rock. Some had a building with rooms built over the top. One room was used as a chapel for the dead.

All the tombs served the same purpose. They had to protect the remains of the dead person and his or her possessions from sandstorms, robberies, and other disasters.

Offerings to the dead

Outside many tombs were special stone tables where food, drink, or other offerings could be left for the mummy's ka.

A priest, or a relative of the dead person, would pray for the offerings to be accepted. The words of the prayers were carved on stone slabs around the tomb.

Mastaba

Types of tombs

Around 5,100 years ago nobles were often buried in underground rooms below walled buildings. These are called mastaba tombs.

Mud-brick walls

Underground burial chamber

Around 4,650 years ago huge pyramids were built above the pharaohs' tombs. The most famous are at Giza, west of the Nile river.

Pyramid

Temple

Sarcophagus

Around 3,570 years ago kings were buried in secret tombs, carved out of the rocky cliffs in the Valley of the Kings, near Thebes.

Rock tomb

Well (to drain water and trap robbers)

Sarcophagus

Underground burial chamber

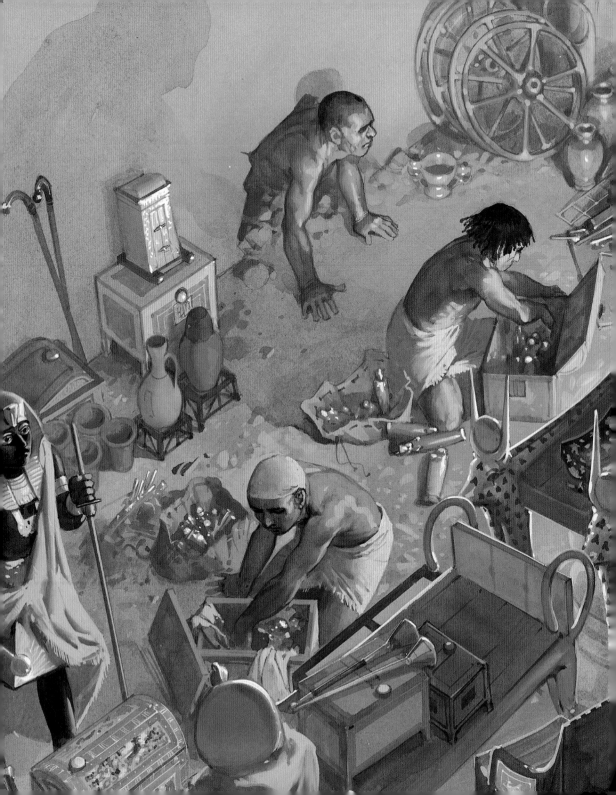

Robbers!

Robbers are breaking into a royal tomb in the Valley of the Kings. They have crept past the guard and have tunneled down to the burial chamber. They are nervous. They may still fall into one of the wells built into the tomb's passageways. And if they are caught, they will probably be killed. But if they can escape with even a tiny gold statue, they will be able to live in comfort for the rest of their lives.

Mummy magic
During the Middle Ages, people in Europe used stolen bits of mummies to make medicines.

Treasure hunters
When French soldiers invaded Egypt 200 years ago, treasure hunters dug up many mummies.

A new tomb

In 1908 some pots and cloth were found in the Valley of the Kings, close to the ancient city of Thebes. They had been used to prepare the mummy of the pharaoh Tutankhamen. But where was his tomb?

In 1922 the archaeologist Howard Carter found the entrance to the tomb. When his employer, Lord Carnarvon, arrived, they broke into the first room.

Inside they discovered stacks of golden treasures. It had been disturbed by robbers, but there were still more than 600 items.

Carter was very excited about this discovery. But he and his team had to work slowly and carefully.

Every item in the chamber had to be photographed, measured, and listed before it was removed.

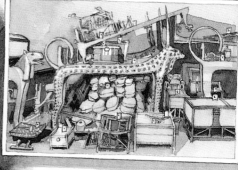

All the statues, boxes, and pieces of furniture were then taken away one by one. It took several years to clear the tomb.

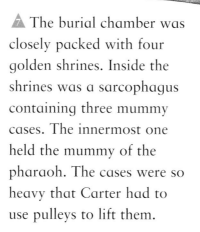

Would the next room hold the 3,500-year-old mummy of Tutankhamen? The king of Egypt himself watched as Carter opened the burial chamber. Inside they saw a wall of gold.

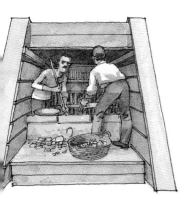

The burial chamber was closely packed with four golden shrines. Inside the shrines was a sarcophagus containing three mummy cases. The innermost one held the mummy of the pharaoh. The cases were so heavy that Carter had to use pulleys to lift them.

Plan of the tomb

Carter had two more rooms to explore. Both were full of treasures. Tutankhamen was not a famous king, but his tomb was an exciting find because his burial chamber had not been robbed.

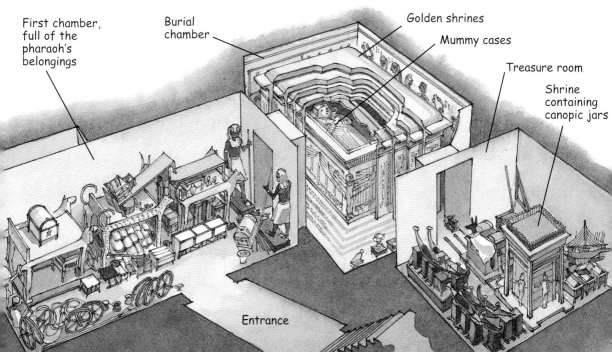

First chamber, full of the pharaoh's belongings

Burial chamber

Golden shrines

Mummy cases

Treasure room

Shrine containing canopic jars

Entrance

Mummies and science

Since the days of Howard Carter, scientists have been able to discover more and more about mummies. Today, scientists can take a small tissue sample from a mummy, such as a piece of bone or skin, and figure out who its relatives were or whether it had any diseases.

Dating a mummy

Scientists can figure out accurate dates from cloth and the wood in coffins and mummy tags.

Mummy tags— found on some mummies

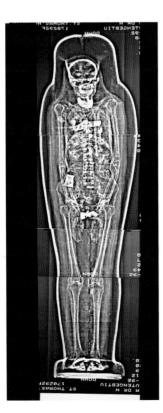

Scanning a mummy

When a hospital needs to see inside someone's body, it may use a scanner. Scanners are now used to examine mummies, too, without having to remove all their bandages.

From scans, scientists can study how the mummy was bandaged, what kind of amulets were used, and whether the mummy had any broken bones.

The last meal

Scientists can examine the stomach and intestines of a mummy to find out what it ate just before it died.

Duck

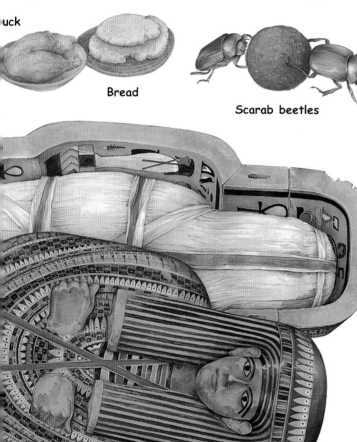

Bread

Beetles and bugs

Tiny bugs found in a mummy's coffin tell us what kinds of insects lived in ancient Egypt.

Scarab beetles

Model of a mummy

Sometimes it is hard to imagine a mummy as a living, breathing person. But experts can make a model of a mummy's head by studying its skull. For example, scientists discovered that one mummy had a broken nose because of the way the bone had healed. Models like this show us what the person looked like thousands of years ago.

Flowers

Lotus flower—
often used in
necklaces and
wreaths

Scientists know what time of year someone died from dried flowers in their tomb.

Glossary

amulet A charm that is believed to protect its wearer from evil.

archaeologist Someone who digs up and studies ancient ruins and remains.

Book of the Dead A group of around 200 spells to help the dead person in the Next World.

canopic jar A container that held the embalmed internal organs (stomach, liver, intestines, and lungs) of a dead person. In the Middle Kingdom the lids of the jars had human heads. By the New Kingdom the lids were made to look like the heads of the four sons of the god Horus—man, baboon, jackal, and hawk.

chamber A small room.

crook and flail Scepters of the god Osiris. Also used by the pharaohs.

embalmer Someone who treats dead bodies so they do not rot away.

hieroglyphs One of the ways of writing used in ancient Egypt. Made up of tiny pictures and symbols.

jackal A wild dog found in Africa and Asia.

ka The force or spirit that the ancient Egyptians believed lived on after the body died.

mastaba An early type of ancient Egyptian tomb, containing an underground chamber, buildings, and a wall.

Middle Kingdom The second of three great periods of ancient Egyptian history, from 1991 to 1786 B.C. During this period, Egypt conquered Nubia and became a stong trading power.

natron Natural mineral salt, found in old lake beds in ancient Egypt, and used in embalming.

necropolis An area where dead bodies were embalmed and buried.

New Kingdom The third of three great periods of ancient Egyptian history, from 1570 to 1070 B.C.

During this period, the pharaohs Tutankhamen and Ramses II reigned.

Next World The place where a person's spirit or soul went after they had died.

Old Kingdom The first of three great periods of ancient Egyptia history, from 2686 to 2181 B.C. The pyramids at Giza were buil during this period.

Opening of the Mouth A ceremony in the ancient Egyptia burial service. It involved touching the mummy with a special tool to open the mouth and give the power of speech an movement back to the mummy.

pharaoh A ruler of ancient Egypt.

pyramid A large pointed or stepped-sided building marking the tomb of a pharaoh.

sarcophagus A large stone box in which a coffin was placed.

scarab A type of beetle, sacred to the ancient Egyptians.